RAINY DAYS
Arts & Crafts

PAPER CRAFT

DENNY ROBSON

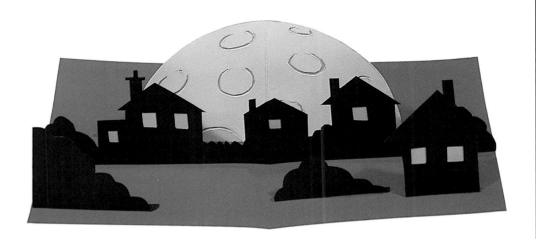

WATTS BOOKS
London • New York • Sydney

CONTENTS

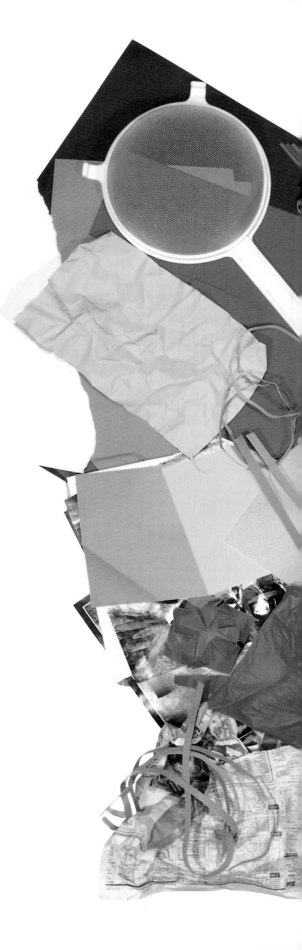

Design: David West
Children's Book Design
Designer: Keith Newell
Photography: Roger Vlitos

© Aladdin Books Ltd 1993

Created and designed by
N.W. Books
28 Percy Street
London W1P 9FF

First published in
Great Britain in 1993 by
Watts Books
96 Leonard Street
London EC2A 4RH

ISBN 0 7496 1305 X

A CIP catalogue record for this book
is available from the British Library

Printed in Belgium

Introduction

This book is full of all sorts of papercraft ideas for you to make. It shows you how to create a dragon puppet by making a paper 'spring'. It introduces you to the traditional Japanese craft of origami. You can find out how to make a collage, pop-up cards, three-dimensional pictures and much more.

Some of the projects are quite simple and can be quickly made. Others will take more time and patience. Papercraft is fun and rewarding, and one of its great advantages is that you don't need a lot of expensive equipment.

When you have tried some of these ideas, why not design your own projects, adding your own ideas to what you have learned?

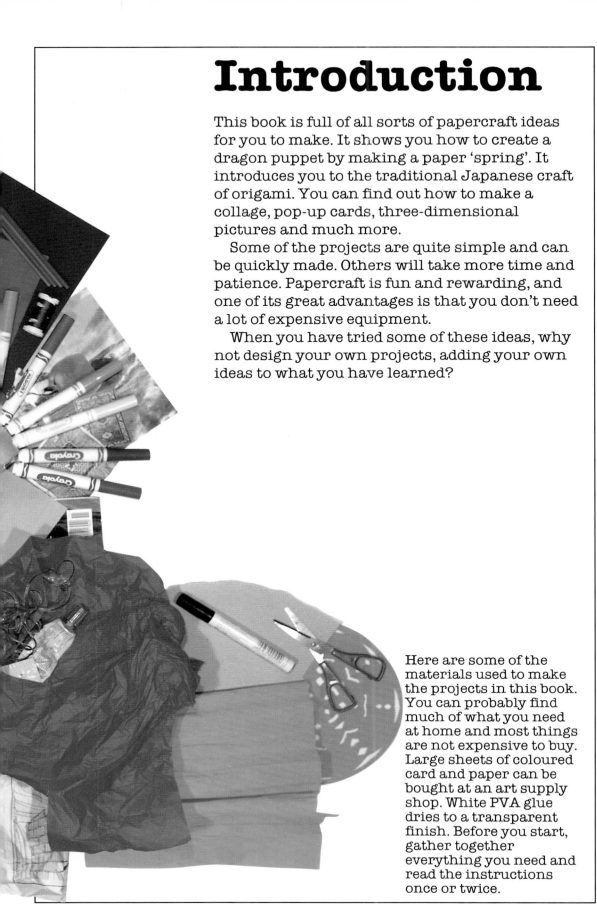

Here are some of the materials used to make the projects in this book. You can probably find much of what you need at home and most things are not expensive to buy. Large sheets of coloured card and paper can be bought at an art supply shop. White PVA glue dries to a transparent finish. Before you start, gather together everything you need and read the instructions once or twice.

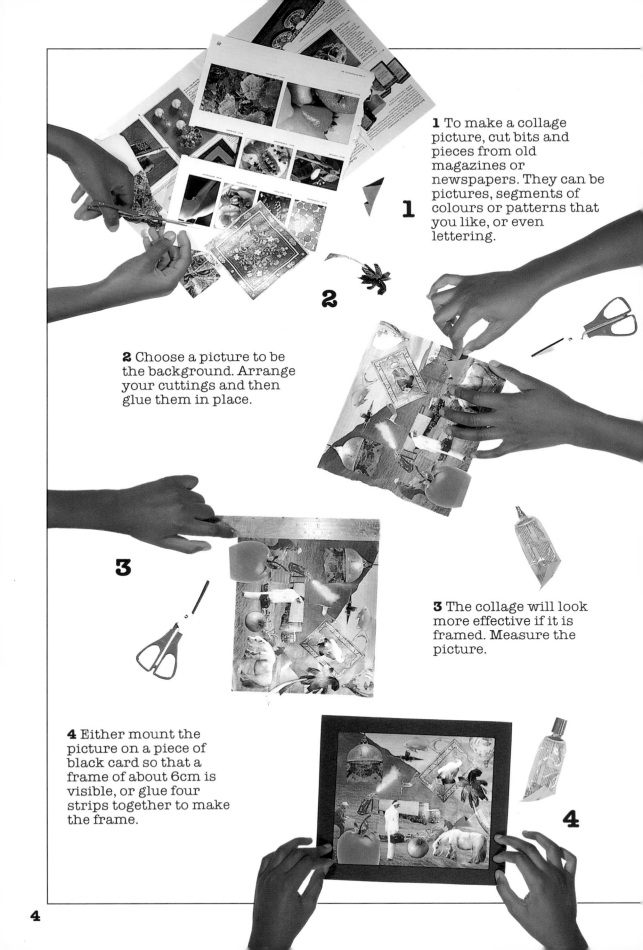

1 To make a collage picture, cut bits and pieces from old magazines or newspapers. They can be pictures, segments of colours or patterns that you like, or even lettering.

1

2

2 Choose a picture to be the background. Arrange your cuttings and then glue them in place.

3

3 The collage will look more effective if it is framed. Measure the picture.

4 Either mount the picture on a piece of black card so that a frame of about 6cm is visible, or glue four strips together to make the frame.

4

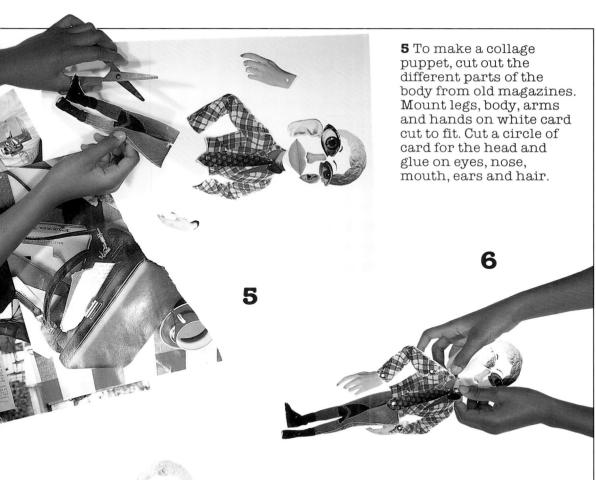

5 To make a collage puppet, cut out the different parts of the body from old magazines. Mount legs, body, arms and hands on white card cut to fit. Cut a circle of card for the head and glue on eyes, nose, mouth, ears and hair.

5

6

6 Using a pencil point to make the holes, fit the puppet together with paper fasteners.

7

7 Glue a straw to the back of the puppet. Its legs, arms, hands and head should move as you twist the straw.

Paper collage

The word collage comes from the French *coller*, which means to glue. The craft of collage is used to describe anything that can be stuck on a background. You don't have to be good at painting or drawing, and as there are no rules, it's a great way to create something impressive and original.

You will need old magazines or newspapers, scissors, glue, white and black card, pencil, paper fasteners, drinking straw.

Book jacket

A collage which has been varnished can make an original and effective book jacket. As well as hunting for cuttings in old magazines, try travel brochures, old postcards and photographs. Experiment with your composition. A great advantage of collage is that you can change your mind lots of times before you decide on the final arrangement.

You will need cuttings, thin white card, scissors, glue, clear varnish and brush, white spirit to clean the brush.

1 Open the book to be covered and lay it on a large sheet of white card. Mark the size of the cover, allowing an additional 6cm at each end to fold inside the book.

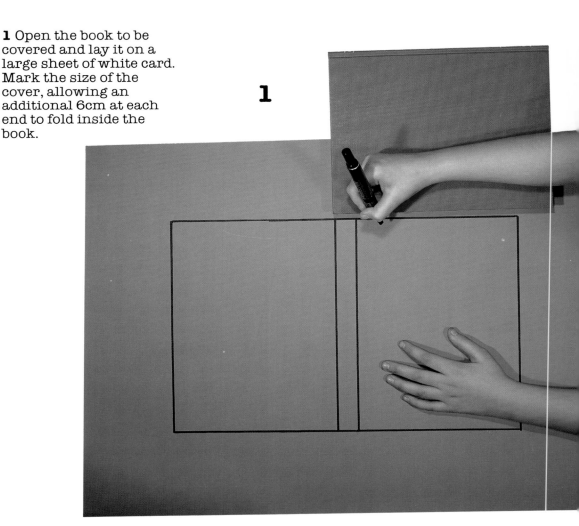

1

2

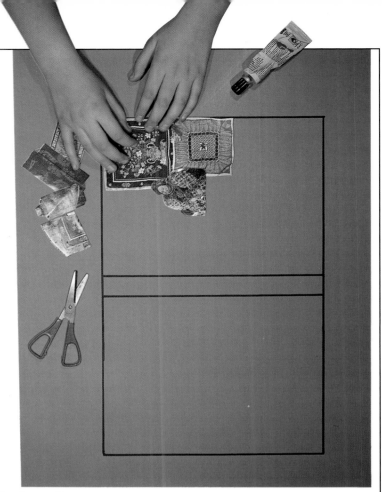

2 Having decided on the arrangement of the collage, (you may want to sketch it out first), glue the cuttings to the card. Make sure that all of the white card is covered.

3 Varnish the collage. This gives the book jacket a strong, glossy finish.

3

4 Finally, trim the corners and fold the jacket around the book.

4

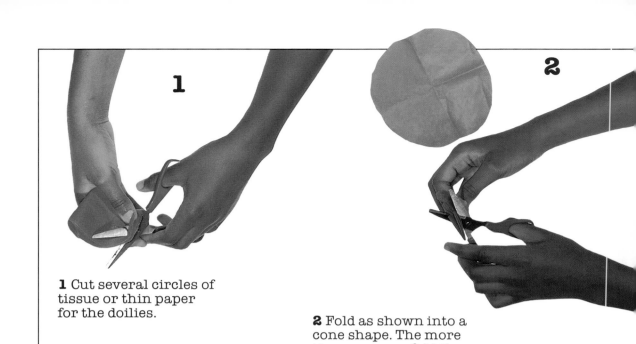

1 Cut several circles of tissue or thin paper for the doilies.

2 Fold as shown into a cone shape. The more times you can fold the paper, the more intricate the design will be. Cut small shapes from the sides.

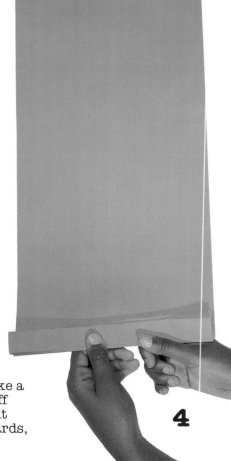

3 Open out the doily and see what kind of design you have created. Experiment with cutting different shapes.

4 To make the fan, take a rectangle of fairly stiff coloured paper. Fold it backwards and forwards, to make pleats.

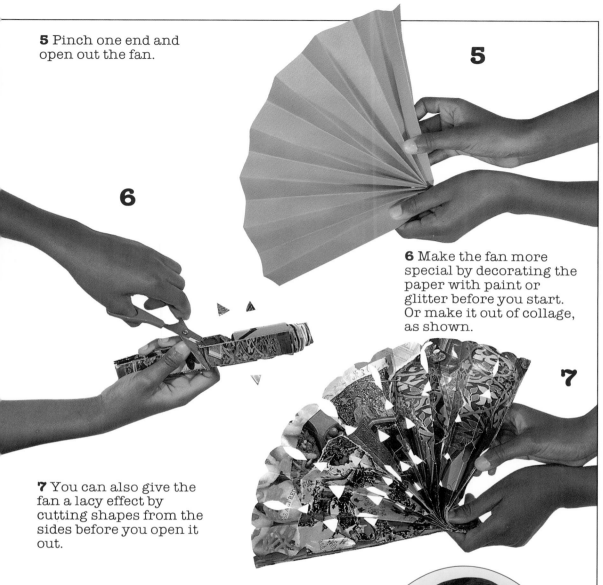

5 Pinch one end and open out the fan.

6 Make the fan more special by decorating the paper with paint or glitter before you start. Or make it out of collage, as shown.

7 You can also give the fan a lacy effect by cutting shapes from the sides before you open it out.

Fans and doilies

Fans and doilies are pretty and effective examples of papercraft that can be made quickly and easily. You can use the doilies to decorate the table at a party. They also look pretty stuck to a window, or you could make a mobile out of them. You can create a special fan by making it out of collage.

You will need coloured paper, scissors, cuttings, glue.

1 Take a square of coloured paper. Using a point of the scissors and a ruler, (you may need the help of an adult), make several evenly spaced parallel cuts, stopping 2cm from each edge.

2

2 Take strips of paper of a contrasting colour and weave them in and out of the paper as shown.

Weaving

All the projects shown here involve weaving. You can make unusual pattern pictures, using lots of different coloured strips and a scored sheet of paper. Or by using the basic weaving technique shown opposite, you can make anything from a plant holder to this crazy hat!

You will need coloured paper, card and tissue, scissors, straws, glue, sticky tape.

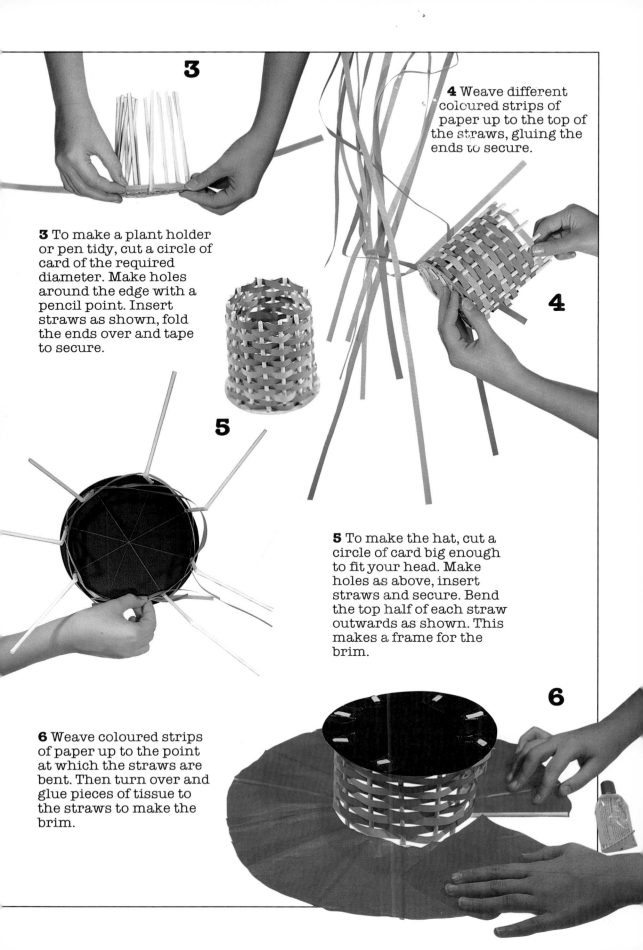

3

3 To make a plant holder or pen tidy, cut a circle of card of the required diameter. Make holes around the edge with a pencil point. Insert straws as shown, fold the ends over and tape to secure.

4 Weave different coloured strips of paper up to the top of the straws, gluing the ends to secure.

4

5

5 To make the hat, cut a circle of card big enough to fit your head. Make holes as above, insert straws and secure. Bend the top half of each straw outwards as shown. This makes a frame for the brim.

6

6 Weave coloured strips of paper up to the point at which the straws are bent. Then turn over and glue pieces of tissue to the straws to make the brim.

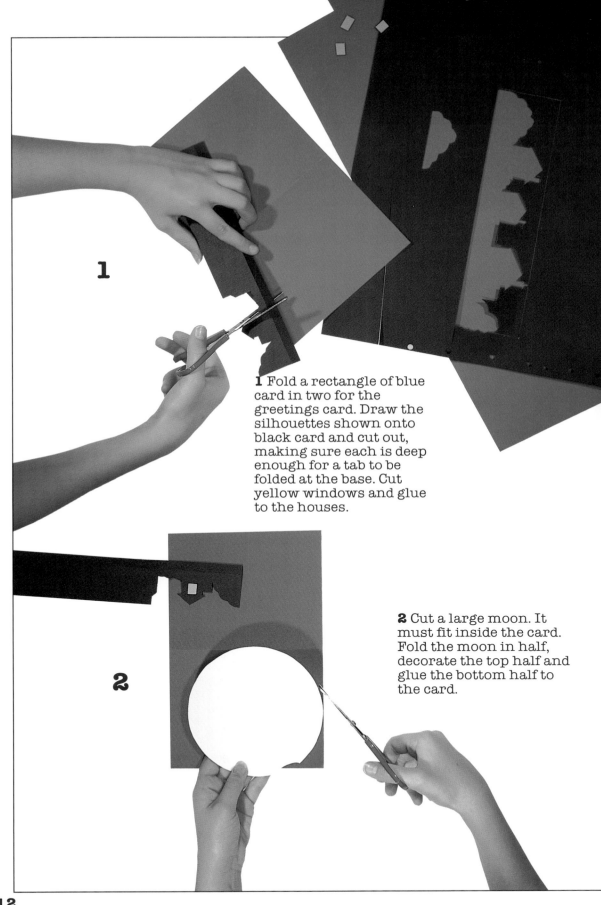

1 Fold a rectangle of blue card in two for the greetings card. Draw the silhouettes shown onto black card and cut out, making sure each is deep enough for a tab to be folded at the base. Cut yellow windows and glue to the houses.

2 Cut a large moon. It must fit inside the card. Fold the moon in half, decorate the top half and glue the bottom half to the card.

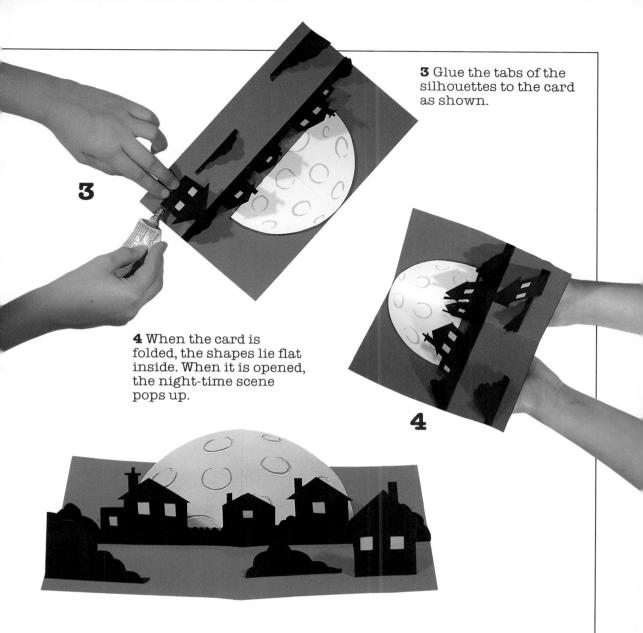

3 Glue the tabs of the silhouettes to the card as shown.

3

4 When the card is folded, the shapes lie flat inside. When it is opened, the night-time scene pops up.

4

Pop-up cards

Greetings cards that pop up when you open them are always fun to make and receive. This day and night card is decorated on the outside with a sun. When you open it, a town silhouetted against a large moon pops up. Pop-up cards are easy to make. Once you've mastered the idea, try making cards of your own design.

You will need thin card — blue, white, black and yellow, pencil, scissors, glue.

1 Cut a circle of card. Decide how to arrange your cuttings and then glue them to the card. Trim the edges.

2 Varnish the collage to give it a strong, glossy finish. Wait until the varnish is dry if you want to give it a second coat.

3 Turn it over, mark pieces and cut. For simple puzzles, cut into just a few large shapes. To make it more difficult, cut into many, irregular pieces.

4 Now try to put the puzzle back together!

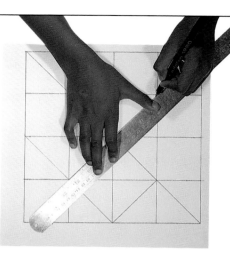

5 This puzzle is made up of different coloured geometric shapes. Draw a grid as shown and divide it into squares and triangles.

5

6

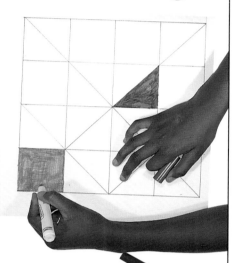

6 Colour each piece, either with paint or felt pens, or glue coloured paper to the card.

7

7 Cut out, mix up the pieces, and then see how quickly you can put them back together again!

Paper puzzles

You can make these puzzles as simple or as complicated as you like. They can be designed so that the difficulty lies in reassembling the shapes. Or you could make a picture, either collage or painted, cut it into pieces and then try to reconstruct it like a traditional jigsaw.

You will need card, cuttings, scissors, glue, pencil, ruler, coloured paper, paints or felt pens.

Dragon puppet

This dragon puppet is great fun to make and play with — it turns and twists as you move its strings. The body is made by the careful folding of a strip of paper. Once you have mastered this technique, you could use it to make up creatures of your own design.

You will need coloured paper, pencil, ruler, scissors, glue, cocktail stick, two straws, cotton thread.

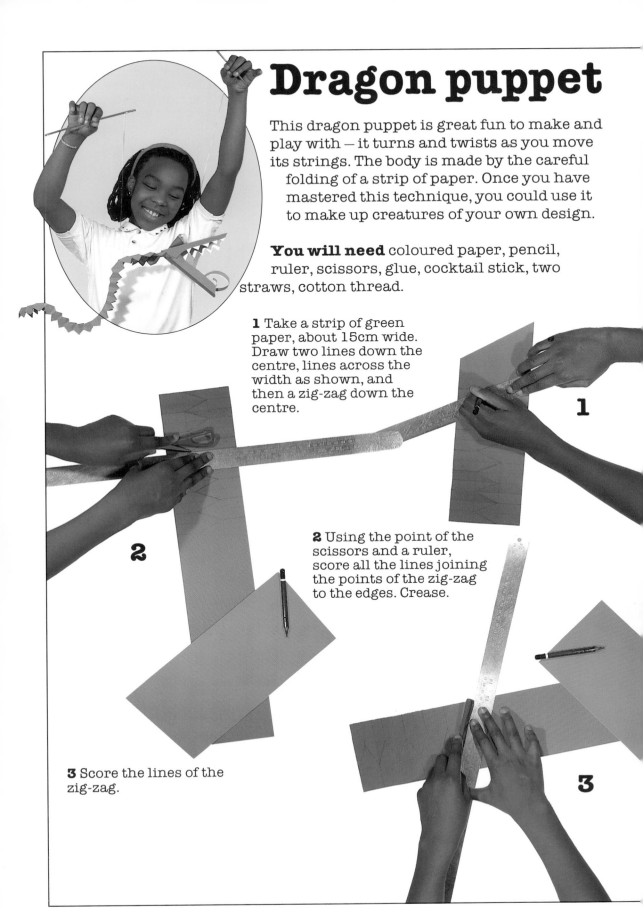

1 Take a strip of green paper, about 15cm wide. Draw two lines down the centre, lines across the width as shown, and then a zig-zag down the centre.

2 Using the point of the scissors and a ruler, score all the lines joining the points of the zig-zag to the edges. Crease.

3 Score the lines of the zig-zag.

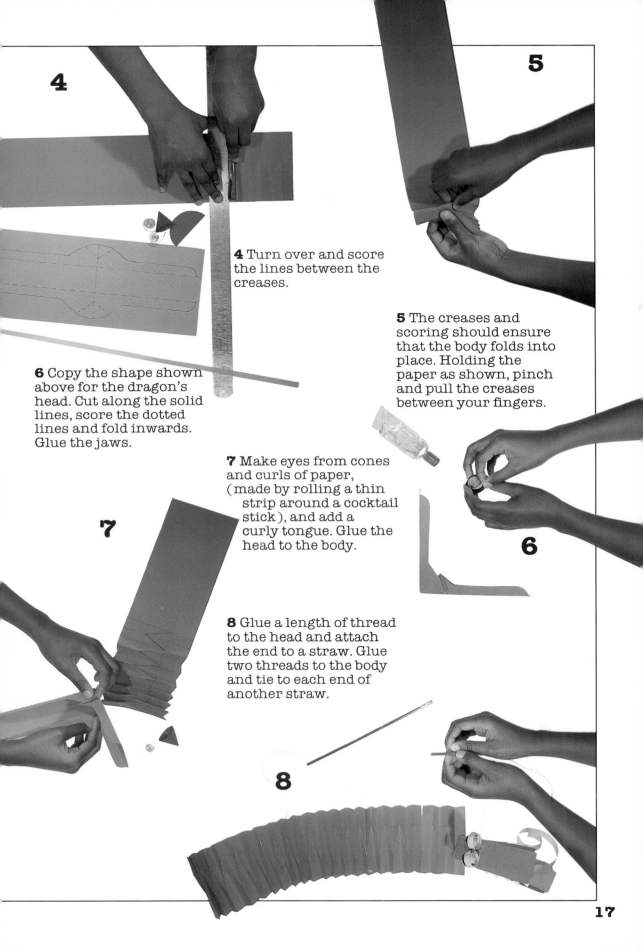

4 Turn over and score the lines between the creases.

5 The creases and scoring should ensure that the body folds into place. Holding the paper as shown, pinch and pull the creases between your fingers.

6 Copy the shape shown above for the dragon's head. Cut along the solid lines, score the dotted lines and fold inwards. Glue the jaws.

7 Make eyes from cones and curls of paper, (made by rolling a thin strip around a cocktail stick), and add a curly tongue. Glue the head to the body.

8 Glue a length of thread to the head and attach the end to a straw. Glue two threads to the body and tie to each end of another straw.

Spinners and tops

Spinners and tops have been popular toys for centuries. One of the earliest optical toys was a spinner called a thaumatrope — a spinning disc with pictures either side that merge as you spin them. Different patterns give different effects as they spin, so experiment with your designs.

You will need card, scissors, straws, coloured paper, felt pens, glue, thin string.

1

1 To make the tops, cut out several circles of card, about 8cm in diameter. Make a pattern on one side either with coloured paper or pens.

2 Make a hole at the centre using a pencil point. Cut a plastic straw in half and insert through the hole.

2

3

3 Spin the top. Here the red and blue merge to give purple. What kind of effects can you create?

4 You can make many different kinds of spinners and tops. To make the spinner on the far right, you decorate both sides of the disc.

4

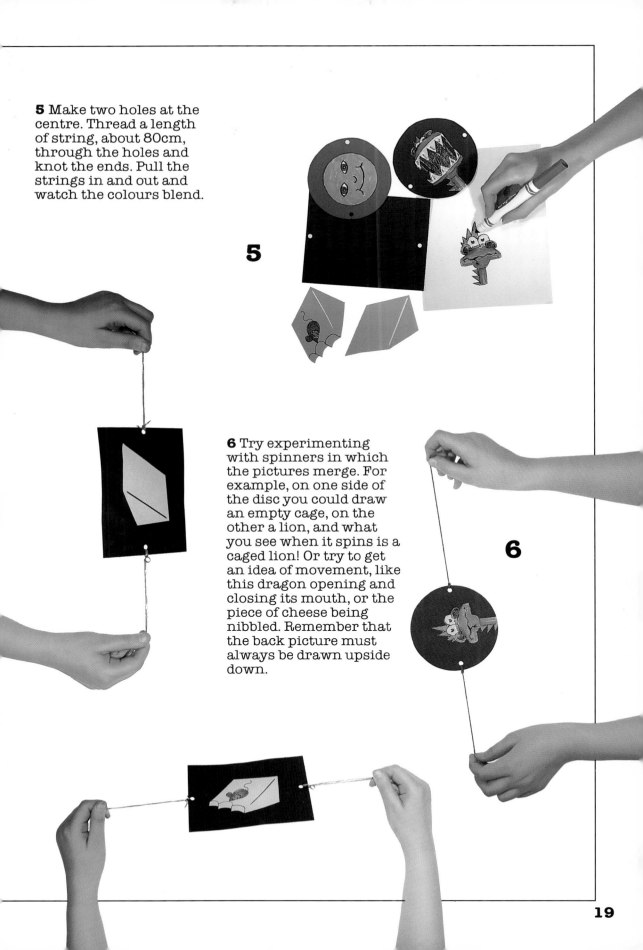

5 Make two holes at the centre. Thread a length of string, about 80cm, through the holes and knot the ends. Pull the strings in and out and watch the colours blend.

5

6 Try experimenting with spinners in which the pictures merge. For example, on one side of the disc you could draw an empty cage, on the other a lion, and what you see when it spins is a caged lion! Or try to get an idea of movement, like this dragon opening and closing its mouth, or the piece of cheese being nibbled. Remember that the back picture must always be drawn upside down.

6

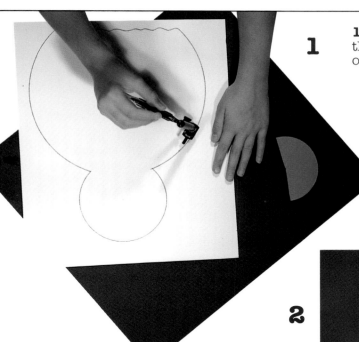

1 Draw the outline for the snowman and cut it out.

2 Lay the snowman on a piece of black card and draw around it. Cut the snowman shape out of the black card, but about 2cm inside the pencil lines. Glue the snowman over this as shown.

3 To make the snowman's broom, cut a fringe in a length of yellow paper.

Advent calendar

Count down the days to Christmas quite deliciously with this sweet-filled advent calendar. Open the first window on 1 December and continue until you get to Christmas Day.

You will need black, white and coloured thin card or paper, pair of compasses, pencil, scissors, 4 eg gboxes or eggtray, sticky tape, glue, straw, cocktail stick, wrapped sweets.

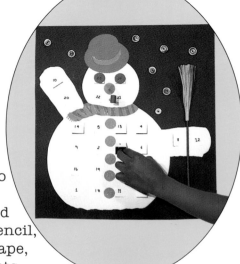

4

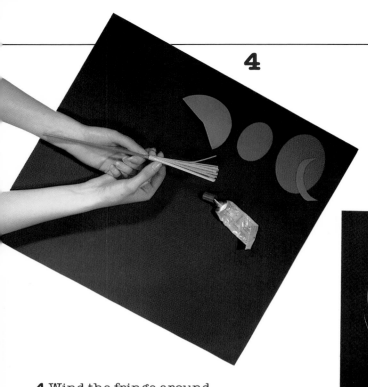

4 Wind the fringe around a straw and glue. Cut shapes for the hat, nose, buttons, eyes, scarf and thin strips of white paper for snow.

5 You need an eggtray or eggboxes with 24 compartments. Arrange as shown. Mark the compartments. Remove the eggboxes, draw a grid and cut 24 windows. Tape the eggboxes back in place.

5

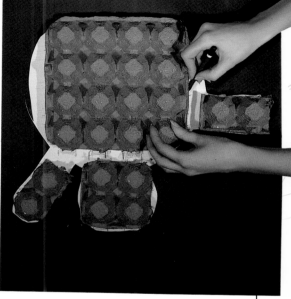

6 Make a cone for the nose and glue decorations to the snowman. You make the snow by winding thin strips of paper tightly around a cocktail stick.

7

6

7 Number the windows 1 – 24, put a wrapped sweet in each compartment and close. As a finishing touch, give the snowman a pipe.

Origami flowers

Origami is the art of folding paper into intricate designs. It is a traditional Japanese craft which is now popular all over the world. The origami flowers shown here can be made into a picture. Turn to page 27 to find out how to make the frame.

You will need squares of coloured paper, card for the background, straws, thin strips of green paper, cocktail stick, glue.

1 Take a square of coloured paper. (This pink paper is green underneath to make it easier for you to see how it folds.) Fold each corner to the centre.

2 Take each corner of this square and fold to the centre.

3 You should now have a smaller square which looks like this.

4 Turn the square over and fold each corner to the centre.

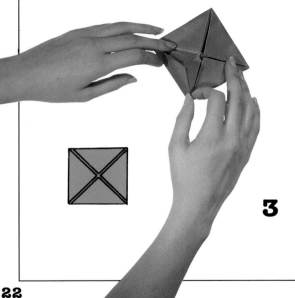

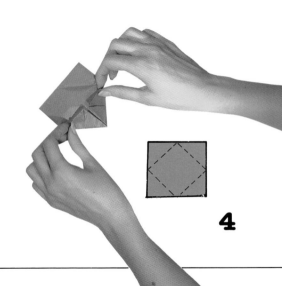

5

5 You should now have an even smaller square which looks like this.

7 Repeat with the other three flaps. Curve each flap up into a petal shape. Repeat with the next four flaps that now become visible.

7

6 Turn the square over. Take one of the four flaps and fold it over the corner as shown. This is the first petal.

6

8 Glue the flowers and straw stems to card. To make the leaves, wind a thin strip of paper tightly around a cocktail stick. Remove and let the roll expand a little. Glue the end in place and pinch the top.

8

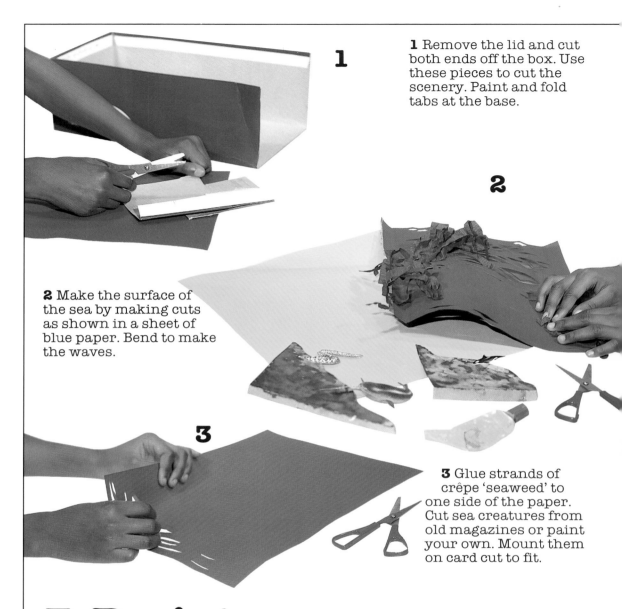

1 Remove the lid and cut both ends off the box. Use these pieces to cut the scenery. Paint and fold tabs at the base.

2 Make the surface of the sea by making cuts as shown in a sheet of blue paper. Bend to make the waves.

3 Glue strands of crêpe 'seaweed' to one side of the paper. Cut sea creatures from old magazines or paint your own. Mount them on card cut to fit.

3-D pictures

Peer into this picture and you can see all kinds of creatures lurking in its depths! This kind of picture is great fun to make. You can use the idea to make any kind of scene you want — deep in a forest, a spooky haunted house, even outer space!

You will need a shoe box, coloured paper or thin card, green crêpe paper, cuttings or drawings of sea creatures, scissors, glue, sticky tape, tracing paper, paints and paint brush.

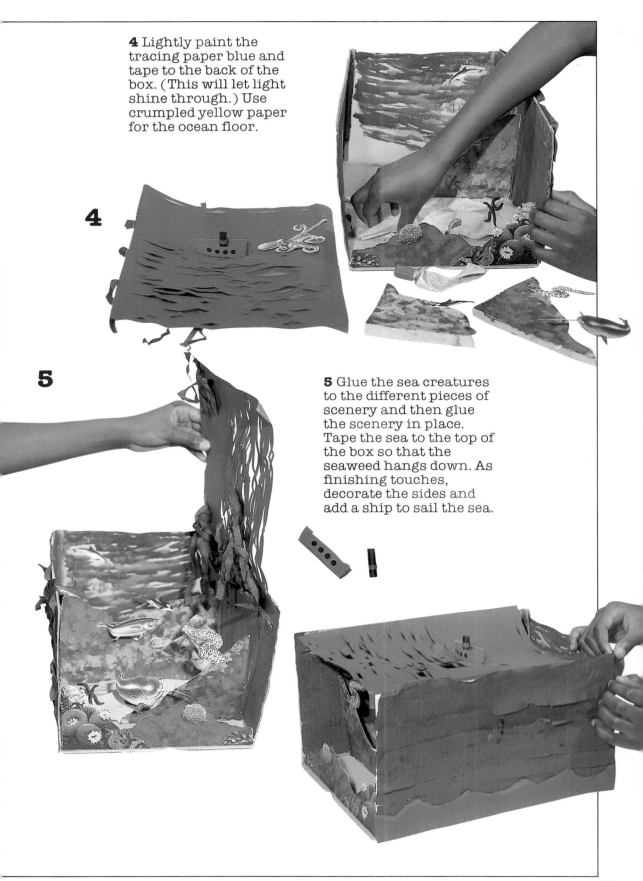

4 Lightly paint the tracing paper blue and tape to the back of the box. (This will let light shine through.) Use crumpled yellow paper for the ocean floor.

4

5

5 Glue the sea creatures to the different pieces of scenery and then glue the scenery in place. Tape the sea to the top of the box so that the seaweed hangs down. As finishing touches, decorate the sides and add a ship to sail the sea.

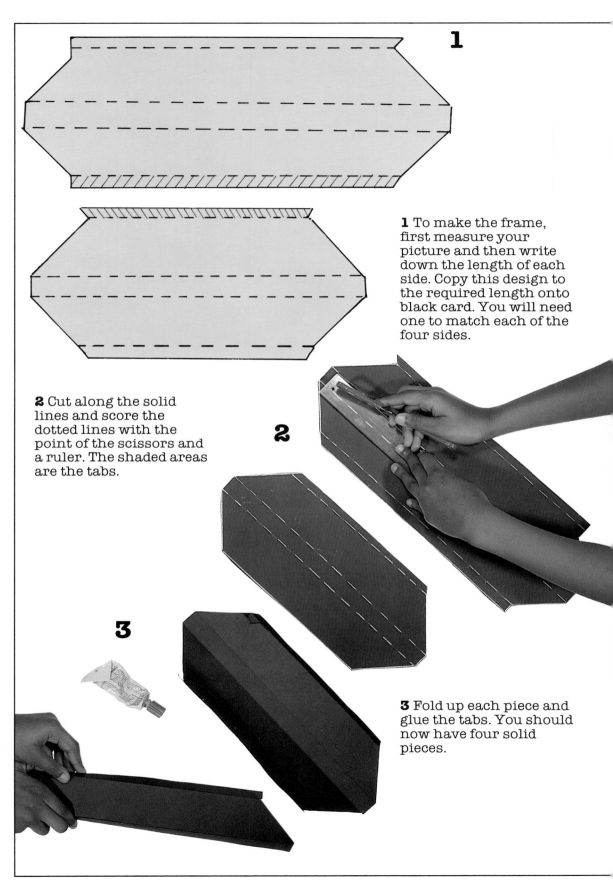

1 To make the frame, first measure your picture and then write down the length of each side. Copy this design to the required length onto black card. You will need one to match each of the four sides.

2 Cut along the solid lines and score the dotted lines with the point of the scissors and a ruler. The shaded areas are the tabs.

3 Fold up each piece and glue the tabs. You should now have four solid pieces.

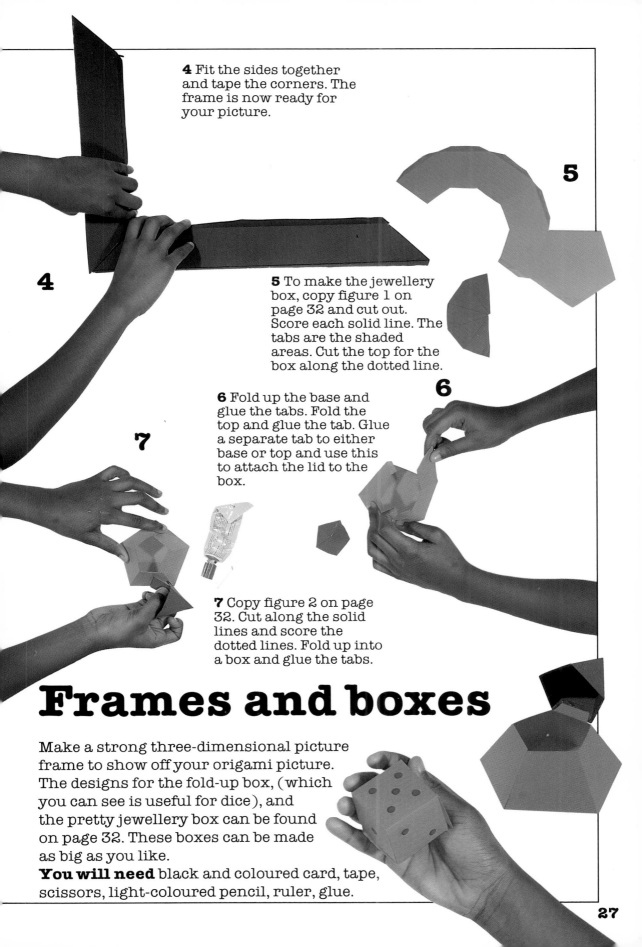

4 Fit the sides together and tape the corners. The frame is now ready for your picture.

5 To make the jewellery box, copy figure 1 on page 32 and cut out. Score each solid line. The tabs are the shaded areas. Cut the top for the box along the dotted line.

6 Fold up the base and glue the tabs. Fold the top and glue the tab. Glue a separate tab to either base or top and use this to attach the lid to the box.

7 Copy figure 2 on page 32. Cut along the solid lines and score the dotted lines. Fold up into a box and glue the tabs.

Frames and boxes

Make a strong three-dimensional picture frame to show off your origami picture. The designs for the fold-up box, (which you can see is useful for dice), and the pretty jewellery box can be found on page 32. These boxes can be made as big as you like.

You will need black and coloured card, tape, scissors, light-coloured pencil, ruler, glue.

1 Cut up old newspapers into a mixing bowl.

1

2 Add water and leave them to soak for a day or so.

2

3

3 Drain off the water and then mix with your hands into a pulp. Soak the pulp in water and then strain through a sieve.

4 Place the pulp onto a dry cloth and spread it out with your hands or a rolling pin.

4

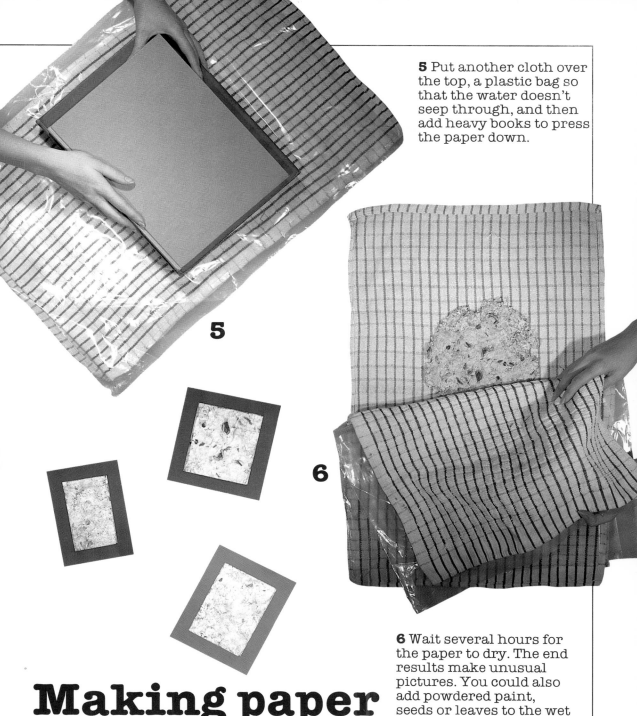

5 Put another cloth over the top, a plastic bag so that the water doesn't seep through, and then add heavy books to press the paper down.

5

6

6 Wait several hours for the paper to dry. The end results make unusual pictures. You could also add powdered paint, seeds or leaves to the wet pulp.

Making paper

Paper was invented in China over 2,000 years ago. It was made from tree bark and wood is still the raw material used in papermaking today. Follow these instructions to find out how you can recycle paper at home.

You will need newspapers, scissors, water, mixing bowl, sieve, tea towels, plastic bag.

Photo panorama

This project is for all budding photographers with a good eye and a steady hand. The idea is to create a panorama of your favourite place. If you view it through this mini telescope, it will seem as if you are actually there!

You will need photographs, stiff card, coloured paper, drinking straw, glue, sticky tape, scissors.

1 Visit an interesting place, such as a park or playground. Take several photographs, moving the camera around the scene, so that each frame slightly overlaps the one before.

2 Mount the developed prints onto card. Now fit the panorama together. Trim the tops and bottoms as needed. Tape the photographs together so that they form a semi-circle.

2

3 The panorama will balance on its own. Make a telescope out of a roll and cone of paper, and use a straw for the stand.

3

4 Position the telescope facing the centre of the panorama. Look through it and you can imagine you're in your favourite place!

4

Box designs

Copy these designs to make the boxes on page 27. They can be made to any size you wish. You may need the help of an adult to calculate the scale.

1

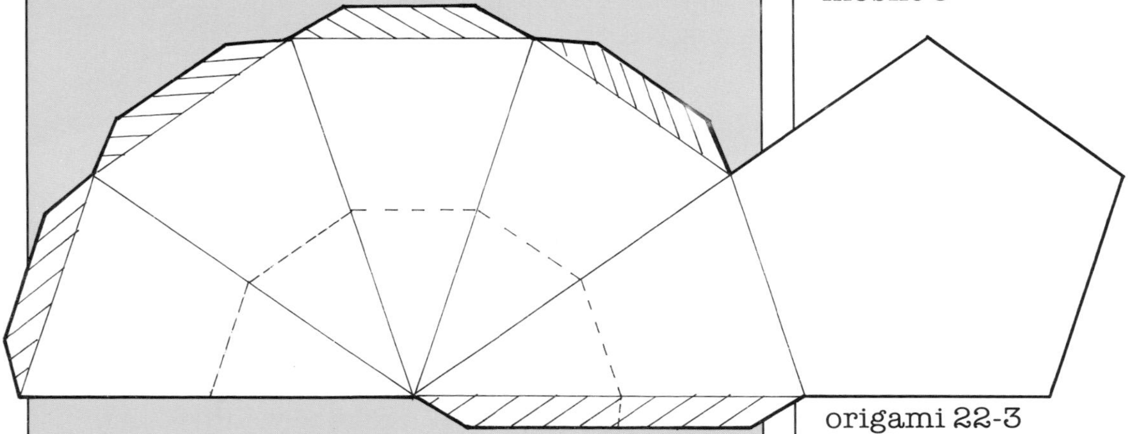

2

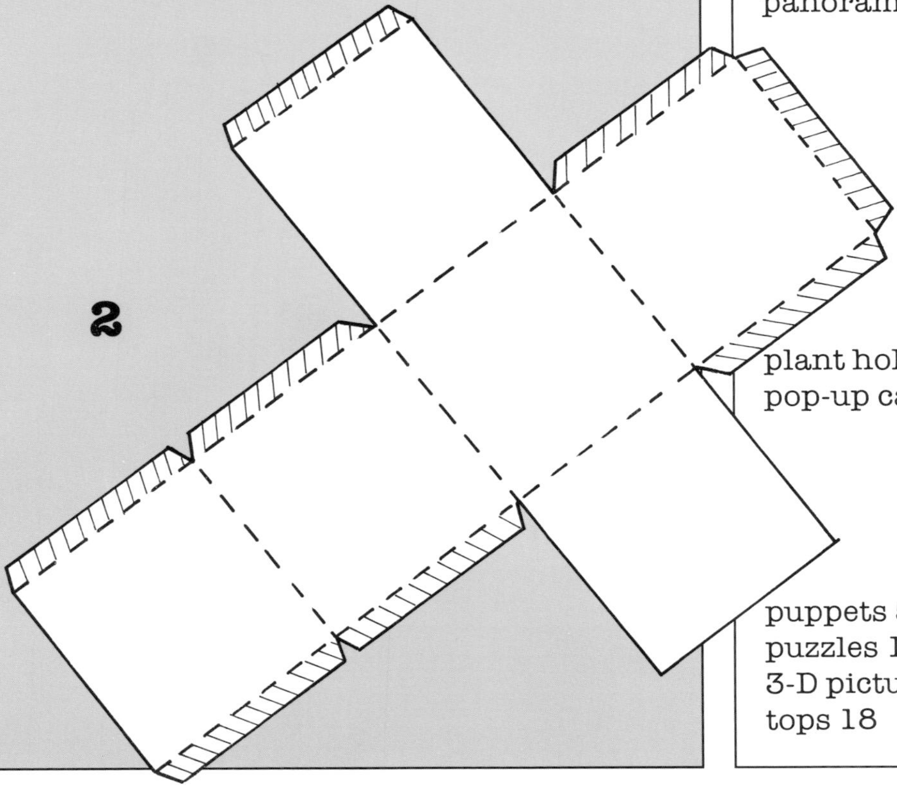